Gathering the Sun

An Alphabet in Spanish and English

Alma Flor Ada

English translation by Rosa Zubizarreta

Illustrated by Simón Silva

LOTHROP, LEE & SHEPARD BOOKS NEW YORK

TO THE LIVING MEMORY OF CÉSAR CHÁVEZ

To my students: María Álvarez, Marta López, Rosario Morales,
Alfonso Anaya, Ricardo Balderas, Frank Espinoza,
Francisco Reveles, and Isidro Tarango,
with gratitude for all they have taught me
about the lives of farmworkers

And to the Zapotec farmworkers from Teotitlán del Valle
—AFA

To my wife María and my sons Josué and Francisco for all the
love and support they have given me

And to Blanca Solis & all the Past, Present, & Future Migrant Workers.
May Their Efforts & Struggles be Respected by all. Viva La Raza!
—SS

Author's Note

By the year 2000, to make it easier for computers to alphabetize text, *Ch* and *Ll* will no longer be considered separate letters in the Spanish alphabet. They have been retained here as unripe fruit, not yet ready to be taken from the tree, since all of us who love our language and the traditions it keeps alive will need some time to grow accustomed to this change.

—Alma Flor Ada

Árboles

Compañeros de mi infancia,
hermosos gigantes verdes.
Ciruelos, peral, pistachos,
durazneros, chabacanos,
almendros, naranjos, kiwi,
cerezos, nogal, manzanos.
Árboles que dan la fruta
que mis padres van pizcando.

Trees

Companions of my childhood,
handsome green giants.
Plums, pears, pistachios,
peaches and apricots,
almonds, oranges, kiwis,
cherries, walnuts, and apples.
Trees that bear the fruits
that my parents harvest.

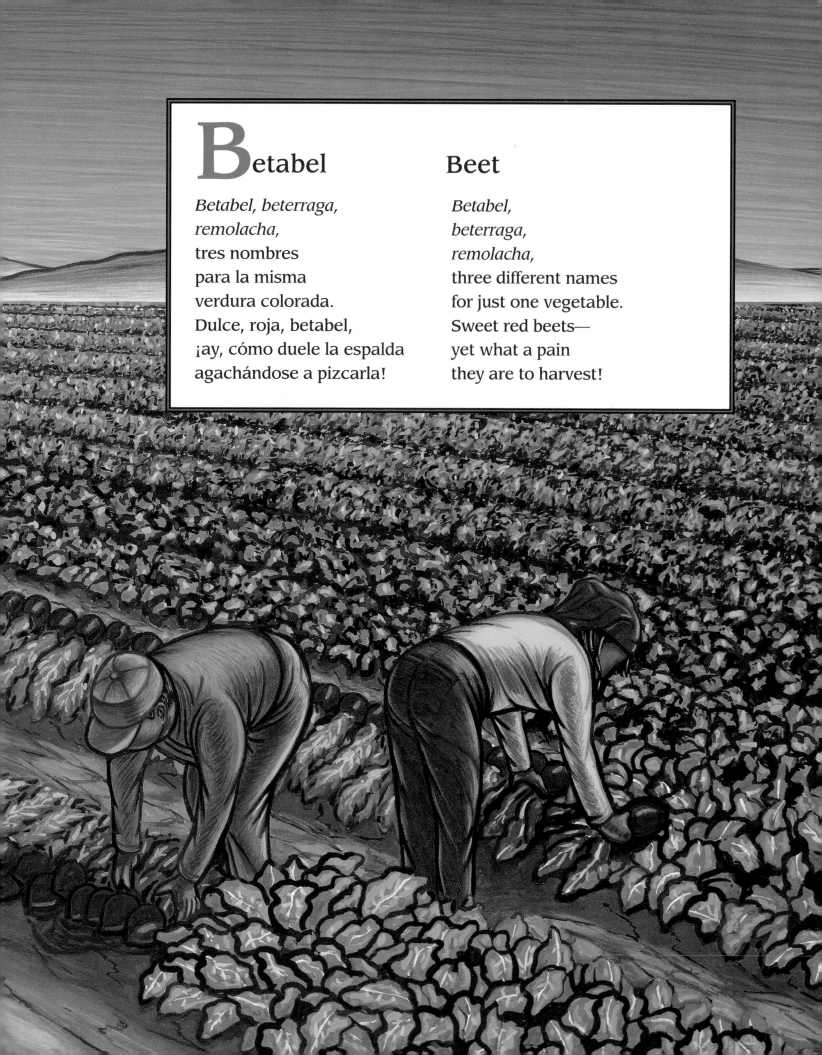

Betabel

Betabel, beterraga,
remolacha,
tres nombres
para la misma
verdura colorada.
Dulce, roja, betabel,
¡ay, cómo duele la espalda
agachándose a pizcarla!

Beet

Betabel,
beterraga,
remolacha,
three different names
for just one vegetable.
Sweet red beets—
yet what a pain
they are to harvest!

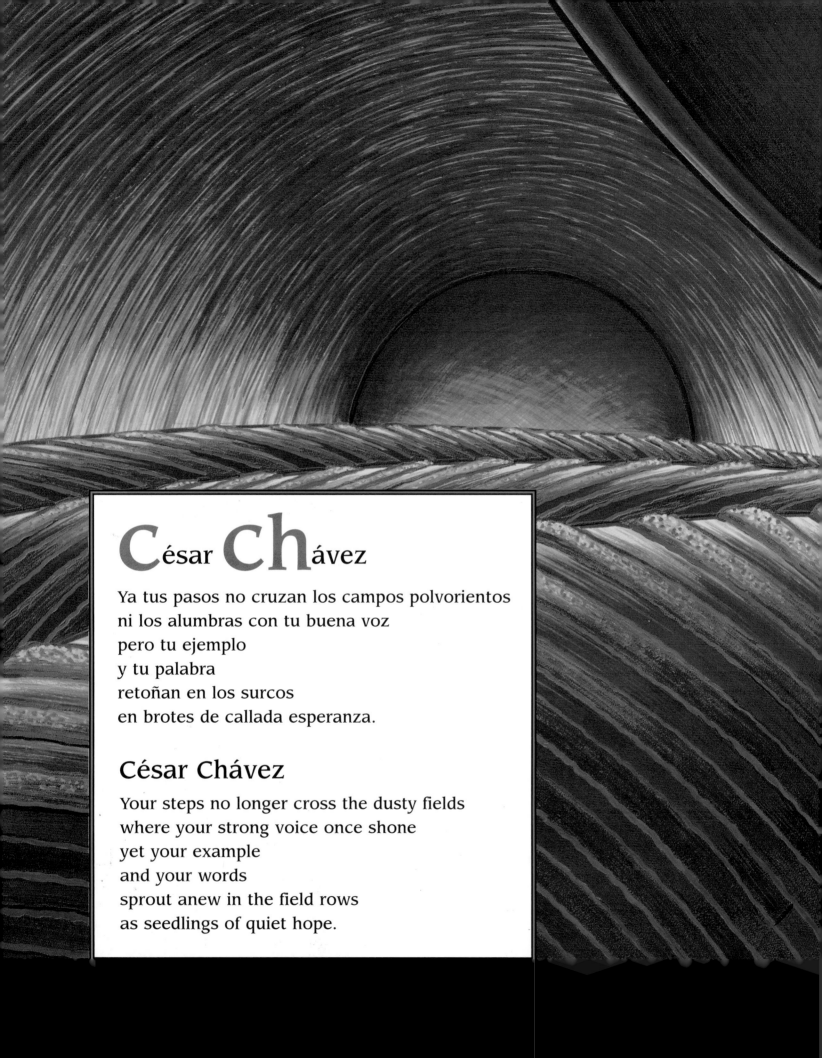

César Chávez

Ya tus pasos no cruzan los campos polvorientos
ni los alumbras con tu buena voz
pero tu ejemplo
y tu palabra
retoñan en los surcos
en brotes de callada esperanza.

César Chávez

Your steps no longer cross the dusty fields
where your strong voice once shone
yet your example
and your words
sprout anew in the field rows
as seedlings of quiet hope.

Duraznos

Duraznos jugosos,
almibarados, dorados,
como una caricia suave
en la palma de la mano.

Peaches

Juicy, golden peaches,
honey-sweet,
like a gentle caress
in the palm of my hand.

¿**E**strellas o **F**lores?   Stars or Flowers?

¿Son las estrellas flores luminosas   Are the stars shining flowers
alegrando la noche?   that brighten the night sky?
¿Son las flores estrellas   Are the flowers drowsy stars
dormidas en los campos?   that lie sleeping in the fields?

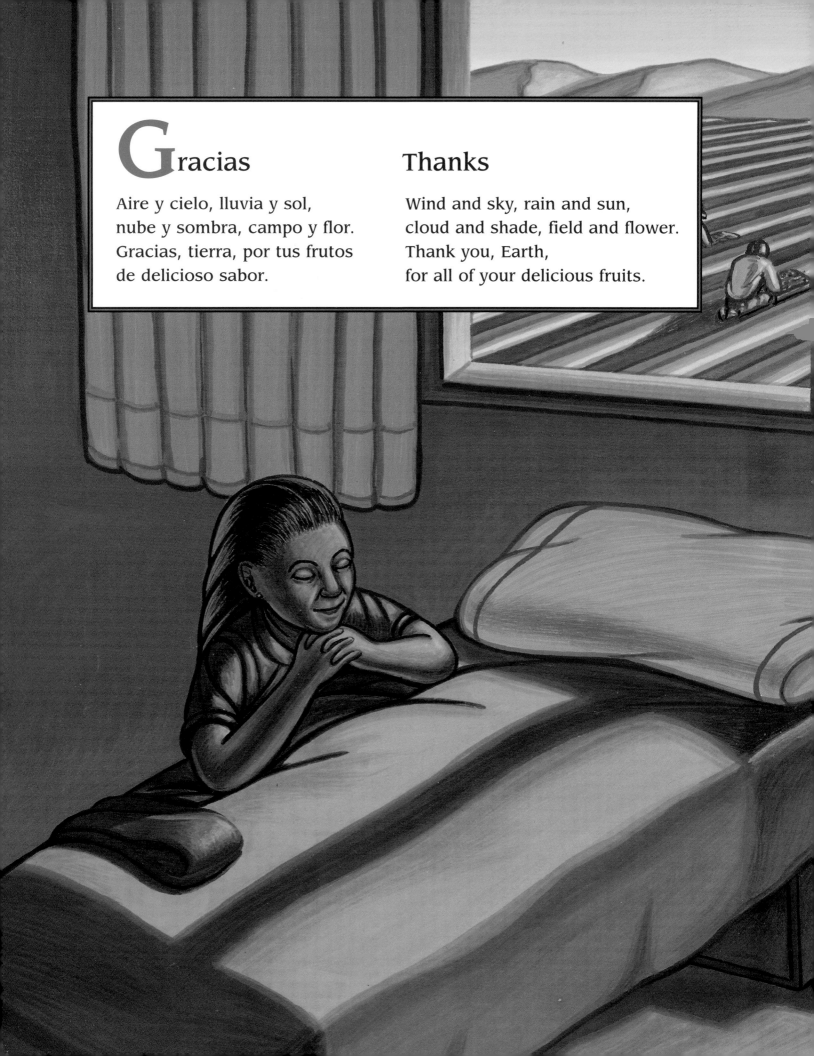

Gracias

Aire y cielo, lluvia y sol,
nube y sombra, campo y flor.
Gracias, tierra, por tus frutos
de delicioso sabor.

Thanks

Wind and sky, rain and sun,
cloud and shade, field and flower.
Thank you, Earth,
for all of your delicious fruits.

Honor

Honor es el trabajo
que hacemos en los campos.
Honor es la familia
que se quiere y se apoya.
Honor es ser quien soy,
al despertar cada mañana.

Honor

Honor is the work
we do in the fields.
Honor is a family
who loves and cares for one another.
Honor is being true to myself
as I wake up each morning.

Isla

Trabaja mi padre bueno
desde que el sol amanece
en las islas del Río Stockton
donde el espárrago crece.

Y cuando el sol ya se pone
en las márgenes del río,
regresa a casa mi padre,
muy cansado, con mi tío.

Island

From when the sun first rises
my good father works
on the Stockton River islands
where asparagus is grown.

And when at last the sun sets
on the river shores,
both my father and my uncle,
very tired, return home.

Jardín

Mi madre trabaja
en un jardín.
Cultiva claveles
blanco y carmín.

Los siembra, los riega
y los transplanta.
Cuando florecen
¡cómo le encantan!

Garden

My mother works
in a garden
growing carnations
both red and white.

Seeding, watering,
and replanting....
And when they bloom,
it's pure delight!

Kiosco de Cerezas

Cerezas en el kiosco
al lado del camino.
Redondas, rojas, lisas,
saludando al que pasa
como sonrisas.

Cherry Stand

Cherries for sale
at a roadside stand.
Round and red,
their smooth smiles
greet everyone who passes by.

CHERRIES

Lechuga

Cabecitas rizadas
llenas de arrugas
frescas, lozanas,
verdes lechugas.

Cajas y cajas
vacías esperan
que doblen las espaldas
quienes las llenan.

Lettuce

Small, curly,
fresh and wrinkled
heads of bright
green lettuce.

Empty boxes
wait for us
to bend our backs
and fill them up.

Lluvia

Plin, plin, plin,
la lluvia suena
como violín.

Borrombombón,
resuena el trueno
como trombón.

Rain

Plink, plink, plink,
the rain sounds like
a violin.

Booroomboomboom,
the thunder is
a deep trombone.

México

De México vinieron
mis abuelos.
A México regresaron
mis padres.
Con ir a México
sueño yo.
Y tú,
¿con qué sueñas?

Mexico

My grandparents
came from Mexico.
My parents
returned to Mexico.
My dream is
to visit Mexico.
And you,
what is your dream?

Nopal

Detrás de sus espinas
el nopal
esconde un fruto dulce.
¡Qué gran sorpresa!

Prickly Pear

Behind the thorns
of the prickly pear,
a sweet fruit is hiding.
Surprise!

Ni Ñ a campesina

Avecita del campo,
es tu sonrisa clara
y tu alegría
la mejor esperanza
del nuevo día.

Field Girl

Little sparrow of the fields,
your open smile
and your joy
are the brightest hope
of the new day.

Orgullo

Orgullosa de mi familia
orgullosa de mi lengua
orgullosa de mi cultura
orgullosa de mi raza
orgullosa de ser quien soy.

Pride

Proud of my family
proud of my language
proud of my culture
proud of my people
proud of being who I am.

Pájaro

Pajarito que vuelas sobre el campo
¿a dónde llevas los sueños
que pongo sobre tus alas?

Bird

Little bird flying over the fields,
where do you take the dreams
I place upon your wings?

Querer

Qué bonito querer a los amigos;
y qué fácil querer a los abuelos;
y el más lindo querer como un capullo,
a los padres querer
y a los hermanos.

Love

How good it is to love our friends;
how easy to love our grandparents;
and the finest blossom of all,
the love we give our parents,
our brothers, and our sisters.

Regar · Watering

Tus sonrisas son
para tus amigos
como el riego
para las plantas.

Your smiles
to your friends
are like water
to growing plants.

Surco

En el surco
la semilla arropada
como el niñito en la cuna.
Duérmete, semilla, hoy.
Despierta, planta, mañana.

Field Row

In the field row
lies a seed, all tucked in
like a baby in the crib.
Sleep tight today, seed.
Wake up tomorrow, plant.

Tomates

Tomatoes

Tomate fresco
en la ensalada,
en la salsa,
en la enchilada.
Tomate rojo
en la cocina,
en los taquitos
de mi madrina.

Fresh tomato
in a salad,
in the salsa,
in enchiladas.
Red tomato
in the kitchen,
in the little tacos
my godmother loves to make.

Uno

No hay una flor
sino muchas, todas de distinto olor.
No hay un fruto
sino muchos, con muy distinto sabor.
No un árbol:
¡cientos de verdes distintos!
Todos en este planeta.

One

Not one flower but many,
each with a different fragrance.
Not one fruit but many,
each with a different flavor.
Not one tree but—
a hundred different shades of green!
All together on this planet.

Violetas

Mis flores un arco iris:
rojas, rosadas,
amarillas, azules
y anaranjadas.
La más preciada,
por su color intenso,
la violeta morada.

Violets

My flowers form a rainbow:
red, pink,
yellow, blue,
and orange.
My favorite,
for its deep hue:
the purple violet.

Farm**W**orkers

Farmworkers nombre en inglés
para el pueblo campesino,
trabajadores del campo,
bajo un mismo cielo unidos.

Gracias te doy, campesino,
por los frutos de tus manos
creceré en fuerza y bondad
comiendo lo que has sembrado.

Farmworkers

Farmworkers is the name we give
to the people who work the land,
who harvest the fields,
united beneath one sky.

Thank you, farmworker,
for the fruits your hands have brought me.
I will grow stronger and kinder
as I eat what you have grown.

Xóchitl

Tu nombre,
que en náhuatl dice flor,
trae aromas lejanos
de la cultura azteca.

Xochitl

Your name,
which in Nahuatl means flower,
carries the distant fragrance
of the rich Aztec culture.

Yucatán

Yucatán,
abrigo verde
del pueblo maya.
En tu selva crecen pirámides,
orgullo de tu ayer y tu mañana.

Yucatan

Yucatan,
green overcoat
of the Mayan people.
In your rain forest pyramids grow,
pride of yesterday and tomorrow.

Zanahoria

Esconde bajo la tierra
su cuerpo, la zanahoria;
porque lo rojo del sol
¡se lo sabe de memoria!

Carrot

The carrot hides
beneath the earth.
After all, she knows
the sun's fiery color
by heart.

The illustrations in this book were done in gouache on Crescent Cold Press Illustration Board.
The display and text type is Leawood Medium set on a Power Macintosh 7500/100.
Production supervision by Cliff Bryant. Designed by Charlotte Hommey.
Printed in Singapore
First Edition   1 2 3 4 5 6 7 8 9 10
Library of Congress Cataloging in Publication Data
Ada, Alma Flor.
Gathering the sun / by Alma Flor Ada; illustrated by Simón Silva.
p.   cm. Spanish and English.
Summary: A book of poems about working in the fields and nature's
bounty, one for each letter of the Spanish alphabet.
ISBN 0-688-13903-5. — ISBN 0-688-13904-3 (lib. bdg.).
1. Children's poetry, Hispanic American (Spanish)
2. Spanish language—Alphabet. 3. Agricultural laborers—Juvenile poetry.
[1. Hispanic American poetry (Spanish) 2. Alphabet.
3. Agricultural laborers—Poetry. 4. Spanish language materials—Bilingual.]
I. Silva, Simón, ill. II. Title. PQ7079.2.A32A64
1997 861—dc20 96-3701 CIP AC